THE JOSHUA GENERATION

by Dr. E. Bernard Jordan

ISBN 0-939241-12-9

The Joshua Generation

2nd Printing

Copyright © 1996 by Bishop E. Bernard Jordan, Zoe Ministries, Church Street Station, P.O. Box 270, New York, NY 10008-0270. All rights reserved. No part of this book may be reproduced in any form without written permission from the author. Printed in the United States of America. Unless otherwise noted, all Scriptures are taken from the King James version of the Holy Bible.

This book is dedicated to my eldest son, Joshua Nathaniel Jordan, for he shall lead with the skill and agressiveness of his namesake, Joshua, in his generation to the glory of God.

In Gratitude

We'd like to give the following individuals a special thank you for their faithfulness and support in helping to make our dream come true:

Rosemary Basu	Minister Don Kelly
Minister Elsa Blake	Jung Ja Kim
Madge E. Boyd	Elder Fitzgerald A. King
in memory of my son Jerome	Bishop George D. Lee III
Thompson	Pastor Connie Miles
Denise J. Bullock	Prophet Charles E. Moore
Marie and Theresse Bynum	Genese L. Muse
Minister Carolyn Coleman &	Amina Prescott
East Baltimore Deliverance	Linda Roebuck
Church	Sara Sanboy
Gaetano Colomba &	Prophets Donald &
Mission with a Vision	Gina Slaughter
Johnya Cross	Rosalind Smith
Pastor Richard Eberiga	Prophetess Connie Williams
Sherille Fagon	Sherron Williams &
Gina Johnson	Karen Cooper

Because of their generosity and obedience to the Spirit of God, we know that they have opened the door for miracles, and we believe that He shall cause the gems of wisdom that are contained within these pages to be made manifest in each of their lives, for the reward of the Lord is sure and addeth no sorrow!

                In His Love and Service,
                Bishop E. Bernard & Pastor Debra Jordan

TABLE OF CONTENTS

AUTHOR'S PREFACE..vii

CHAPTER 1..........A New Generation..........................1

CHAPTER 2..........Crossing Your Jordan....................15

CHAPTER 3..........Possessing the Land.....................23

CHAPTER 4..........A Call to Action............................35

CHAPTER 5..........Men of Valor.................................47

CHAPTER 6..........The Joshua Mentality...................65

CHAPTER 7..........The People's Choice.....................71

AUTHOR'S PREFACE

Hear ye! Hear ye! The battle cry!
For the time of action does draw nigh!
Awaken from slumber--a new day has dawned;
It is time to arise and obey the Son!
Confrontation on every side--
Declare ye the truth in the face of a lie!
Passivity go! Let God's Kingdom come--
For the earth doth travail for God's manifested sons!

This is the hour of confrontation--the time for the Church to awaken from the sleep of passivity and grasp the responsibility which has been placed upon its shoulders. To fulfill the mandate of God , with all of its implications, will require a different mentality than the one we have currently espoused. For this is the season that God is calling for us to embrace the aggressive nature of the Joshua Generation...for we have been given an inheritance that rests in the Promised Land. God's promise to us is "Yea and Amen", but where do we go from here?

THE JOSHUA GENERATION will enlighten you, encourage you, and yes, for some, provoke you to action as you identify and acquiesce to the call that has been placed in your path. This book will challenge you to strive to attain everything that God has promised you, and motivate you to excellence.

Paul tells us to "forget the things which are behind, and press on towards the mark of the high calling in Christ Jesus..." "For it's a new day", saith the Lord! "Open your eyes and see what is waiting for thee upon the horizon---for it is yours! Go and possess your land!!"

Dr. E. Bernard Jordan

Chapter 1
A New Generation

"Now after the death of Moses the servant of the Lord, it came to pass, that the Lord spake unto Joshua the son of Nun, Moses' minister, saying,

Moses my servant is dead; now therefore arise, go over this Jordan, thou, and all this people, unto the land which I do give to them, even to the children of Israel.

Every place that the sole of your foot shall tread upon, that have I given unto you, as I said unto Moses.

From the wilderness and this Lebanon even unto the great river, the river Euphrates, all the land of the Hittites, and unto the great sea toward the going down of the sun, shall be your coast.

A New Generation

> *There shall not any man be able to stand before thee all the days of thy life: as I was with Moses, so I will be with thee: I will not fail thee, nor forsake thee.*
>
> *Be strong and of a good courage: for unto this people shalt thou divide for an inheritance the land, which I sware unto their fathers to give them."*
>
> Joshua 1:1-6

This Scripture is referring to occurrences that took place after the death of Moses, who was the servant of the Lord. Moses fulfilled his course and purpose for his generation. Moses entered into all the fullness that he could have obtained. Now that Moses was dead, God had a different agenda for the nation of Israel.

There is another anointing that is about to be launched in the earth. That which you did with Moses will pass away. You are going to find that when you are moving with the Joshua spirit, it is an entirely different anointing. The Moses company always sought to go back to Egypt. They had a slavery mentality, and feared the unfamiliar. Even after being delivered from the bondage of slavery, their mind-set caused them to yearn for the familiar circumstances that they could easily assimilate. This was the company that could not enter into the promised land. The Joshua company, on the other hand, are fearless and possess a pioneering spirit that precludes

Prophetic Principle #1

Joshua's company is whom God desires to raise up in our generation!

any hesitation in possessing their inheritance.

Verse 2 *"Moses my servant is dead; now therefore arise, go over this Jordan, thou, and all this people, unto the land which I do give to them, even to the children of Israel."*

Even though God will say,"The land is thine," you have to read the small print, because there are some things that you have to do before you can enter and possess the land.

There are some things on the inside of your mind that must die, that must be obliterated. You must slay the old way of thinking that wants to go back into Egypt and embrace captivity. Some of the conversation that flows from your mouth and rests upon your lips must be identified as the deceitful lies of the enemy, and must be cast down for your very survival's sake.

Prophetic Principle #2

Those who bear the Joshua spirit do not dwell upon the past.

A New Generation

You might say, "Well, when I was out in the world I was doing this, or I could have been doing that." This is a significant sign that the Moses generation mentality is reigning big in you! They have reckoned their past failures and successes dead, and live for the vision set before them. As you grow in your experiences with God, you will find that He frequently goes against the grain of your thinking process. He wants to get rid of your stinkin' thinkin'! God is going to eliminate that poverty mentality of lack that cripples your progress. It murmurs in your ear, "You can't make it, and you can't do it."

If you don't learn to supplant this lie with the truth of God's Word, you'll dwell in a quagmire of your own frustration and regret as you're forced to watch the rest of us as we begin to possess the land. You must have the Joshua spirit to possess the land.

The Moses generation said, *"We be not able."* The Moses generation could not see it, or rather, they saw it but could not enter into it. The Moses generation had a grasshopper mentality - they were small minded and bound by small vision. The Joshua company was a company of expansive vision; they progressed from the small mindedness of slavery and began to enlarge in the greatness of the promises of God. They were the generation that was destined to inherit the land that God had promised His people, and so are we!

While others are busy looking for a way out, I'm looking to possess! While others are looking to escape

Joshua Generation

responsibility, I am looking to take over! God has given us an inheritance! When we look at the word "inheritance", we find it is the act of inheriting. To inherit means "To make an heir or to receive a legacy (money or property) left in a will" It is also something resulting and left behind by an action, such as "a successful descendant." God wants you to know that He has left an inheritance with your name on it, for "the earth is the Lord's and the fullness thereof, and they that dwell therein".

Calling Versus Commission

Deuteronomy 34:9, tells us that Joshua, the son of Nun, was full of the spirit of wisdom. How did he get filled with the spirit of wisdom? Verse 9 continues, *"...for Moses had laid his hands upon him."* Because of the laying on of hands, he was filled with the spirit of wisdom. He was anointed. Therefore, we can begin to see his calling versus his commission.

Prophetic Principle #3

Anointing does not produce authority.

Joshua, though anointed, did not have the authority or commission to proceed until after the death of Moses. Sometimes we think that just because we are anointed, the Red Sea should part for us! Our anoint-

A New Generation

ing doesn't mean a thing except to confirm that the call is there. The question that you should consider is, "Am I appointed?" Some of you may argue with this and think, "I am appointed by God---that is all that matters." No. Your appointment is incomplete until God speaks to some authority in the flesh who must point his finger and commission you.

Notice, that Samuel went and anointed David. David was anointed as king, but he did not begin to rule as king until he was appointed by someone and called forth in due season.

In this hour, too many individuals in the Body of Christ have anointing and appointing confused. People are using their anointing as their authority and are moving in a spirit of deception. They are manipulating the people of God with their anointing and they have not been delegated a true measure of authority by God.

How is this so? Well, these renegade prophets will beckon people to come over to them for a minute, get in the corner and start prophesying. They will tell them to lift their hands and prophesy "And yea, the Lord will say that I will bless your family and your home, and I am going to do mighty things in your midst."

They were anointed, but did they have the authority to speak into the lives of individuals? If you don't watch that spirit, before you know it, they will be saying, "Here is my address, we have prayer meetings every Tuesday night at my house..Be there! God has something more that He wants to tell you." These people manipulate others with their anointing, and they do not have true authority. Misused anointing promulgates rebellion, for the individual who is deceived into thinking that his anointing qualifies him for ministry will not willingly submit himself to true oversight since his "anointing" is greater than any "common man's". They fall victim to the sin of pride and eventually experience a great decline and downfall due to their ignorance.

Joshua could not lead the people into the promised land until the time appointed of the Father. Even though he had the wisdom, and mind-set, and was able to declare some forty years earlier, "We be well able. Let us go forth now and possess the land. If you don't want to go, I am leaving you, I am going on." He had to wait until he received his Divine appointment and commission from God. Do not move until you have God's commission that flows through His servant, for it is His seal of approval.

We notice something else about Joshua in verse one: *"...it came to past, that the Lord spake unto Joshua the son of Nun, Moses' minister, saying..."*

Joshua was Moses' minister. The Holy Ghost is asking you, "Whose minister are you?"

And yet again, the impudent voice of rebellion cries out,"Wait just a minute here, I have been told to go

A New Generation

directly to God first."

Whose minister are you?

God looked at Joshua, and He knew Joshua was Moses' minister.

If you are going to be raised up to fulfill any capacity of leadership or to stand in a place of authority, you have to become someone else's minister.

And the impatient one continues to object saying,"No, no, no! I am taking a shortcut. I am just going to be raised up in leadership. I am just going to stay in a room somewhere and fast and pray and seek the face of God."

No! That is not the way you progress to the fullness of ministry! You have to become someone's minister. That Moses complex will say, "Wait a minute, I don't buy that. I am going back into that old mind-set. I only need God."

Joshua had a different spirit. Joshua had the spirit of the man, Moses. He hung around and observed Moses as he handled the various complexities of ministry. He had the patience to allow the wisdom and anointing of God to ferment in his life. Today, people want to pick the time, place, and season in which God is to move in their lives.

I have watched the Spirit of God move throughout congregations upon individuals, giving them the way out. The very thing that presents itself as their deliverance they mistakenly perceive as their enemy. They begin with their excuses and say, "Well, I can't do it because of this, or because of that."

I find that usually, when God tells you to do something, He tells you to do it in an inconvenient season. Don't make the mistake of thinking that when God is speaking, it is going to be at your convenience.

> **Prophetic Principle #4**
>
> **God called His servants at inconvenient times.**

It wasn't Moses' decision to be called into action at the time it happened. Moses could have reasoned, "I am next in line, I am just about to be raised up, Lord. Why don't you wait until I get into office and then call me to be your deliverer when I have power in the government." Yet God has His own agenda.

Again, usually when God starts to talk to you about doing something, He usually stirs you to move in an inconvenient season.

> **Prophetic Principle #5**
>
> **God's timing usually won't coincide with our rationale.**

A New Generation

The rich young ruler said, "*I have kept all the commandments from my youth.*" Jesus said, "*Good. Now take all of your riches, sell them, and give the proceeds to the poor.* And the rich young ruler foolishly replied, "Well, Lord, that's inconvenient."

Philip was preaching in a meeting where God was moving in signs, wonders, and miracles. The Holy Ghost announced that they had to go to the back side of the desert. Philip objected, "God you're moving now?" God said, "Come on to the back side of the desert, Philip, we have to go meet the Ethiopian eunuch." Philip, busy with "the work of the Lord" remonstrated and said, "God, in the height of the revival? You know I am the man with the power for the hour. This move is inconvenient. God, why don't you wait until after the meeting is over and then we will go deal with him later?" Of course, this is stretching the truth a little bit, for the Bible doesn't record that Philip objected. But this is such a good illustration of what our reaction would be if God began to change the agenda we've grown accustomed to. How many of us can boast of absolute and immediate obedience to God's every command?

God stirs you up in your inconvenient season. "My job is giving me more hours now. Pastor, listen, we just can't make it to church. You'll be doing good just to see me in church some Sundays." The call of God has become an inconvenience in your life.

Elijah said to Elisha, "Leave me." It would have

been convenient for Elisha to become offended and say, "Yes, no problem." But, Elisha said, "I will not."

Are you selling out for convenience? "But you don't understand, pastor, it is inconvenient to..." Yes, that is usually when God tells you to give or make a demand upon your life. You have to realize that if you want to receive the miraculous, you have to begin to do the miraculous. You become the initiator of the miracle. God moves on you and waits for you to act so He can respond. That is why everything in life begins with a seed. God is waiting on you.

Prophetic Principle #6

The miraculous begins with you.

Exodus 17:8-14:

"Then came Amalek, and fought with Israel in Rephidim.

And Moses said unto Joshua, Choose us out men, and go out, fight with Amalek: tomorrow I will stand on the top of the hill with the rod of God in mine hand.

So Joshua did as Moses had said to him, and fought with Amalek: and Moses, Aaron, and Hur went up to the top of the hill.

And it came to pass, when Moses held up his

A New Generation

hand, that Israel prevailed: and when he let down his hand, Amalek prevailed.

But Moses' hands were heavy; and they took a stone, and put it under him, and he sat thereon; and Aaron and Hur stayed up his hands, the one on the one side, and the other on the other side; and his hands were steady until the going down of the sun.

And Joshua discomfited Amalek and his people with the edge of the sword.

And the Lord said unto Moses, Write this for a memorial in a book, and rehearse it in the ears of Joshua: for I will utterly put out the remembrance of Amalek from under heaven."

Notice in verse 9, that Moses gave the commission to Joshua to choose the people, and then God told Moses to write it in the book. Moses was also instructed to rehearse it in the ears of Joshua. Moses knew that Joshua had so much of his spirit that he was able to delegate authority to Joshua and that Joshua had the ability to carry out orders, just as if Moses were there.

Prophetic Principle #7

Your degree of service is going to determine your degree of reigning.

Joshua Generation

Every leader needs a Joshua. Every Joshua should be able to communicate to people. When you have a Joshua mentality, you understand that your purpose is to serve.

Exodus 33:11 *"And the Lord spake unto Moses face to face, as a man speaketh unto his friend. And he turned again into the camp: but his servant Joshua, the son of Nun, a young man, departed not out of the tabernacle."* (This occurred before Joshua became a leader in the house of Israel, on the front lines).

We can see that though God spoke to Moses face to face, Joshua made sure that he was in the tabernacle. He didn't want to depart from the presence of God. He wanted to be in position, to be always ready. He remained in the tabernacle, so when God did call him, he was within the range of hearing.

You need to remain close to your leader to serve him and stay in a position to receive from God when He is ready to exalt you.

Chapter 2
Crossing Your Jordan

"Moses my servant is dead; now therefore arise, go over this Jordan.."

Joshua 1:2

God told Joshua to arise and to go over the Jordan. We see a new command given to the new order. In other words, "get up and take action". The word "Jordan" means "descender." Jordan also meant "descending one, the flowing down abundantly, a dispenser from above." Jordan can also be a type of death. He was sending Joshua and the people over Jordan, to go through death to begin life.

You are just looking at the water, but God is saying it is time for you to go down into Jordan. To

Prophetic Principle #8

God is calling some of you to come face to face with death before you can experience true resurrection life.

God is calling you to cross over your Jordan.

cross over your Jordan is also to go down into your subconscious---into the streams of your deepest thoughts. God is saying He wants you to descend very deep and allow Him to pull up everything that is not of Him. Every thought, every idol, and every false image must be exposed to the scrutiny of His Word. He wants to destroy every shackle of slavery that has kept you bound so that you can thrive in the liberty of His Spirit.

Until you go down into your Jordan, into your deep, you will not be able to possess your land. You must cross Jordan. There are some things in your past that you are running from, because you don't want to deal with them. You have swept some things under the carpet and said, "Well, just let that work itself out, just let me be holier than thou now."

God is saying, "I want to bring you to your Jordan. I want to go down to the deep streams of your thoughts. The thing that you feared might come upon you. I want you to face your Goliath."

Women who are saving for that rainy day just in case their husbands should leave, men who are thinking about getting a divorce because they feel it is just not working out; these are people who are crippled by fear and need to go down into the deep and face their Goliath. Go down to Jordan. The fear that is there will keep you out of the promised land.

You have to cross your Jordan. Descending into the subconscious, the lower part of you, that deep self no one sees, which is really the motor that is running your car. The subconscious is that area that God wants to get into and renew, because that is really the energy and the force that keeps you going. It contains whatever has been programmed into you. You need to go down and over your Jordan! Three points concerning that Jordan: **Number 1:** You want to go down and remove the adverse thoughts.

Number 2: When the enemy, or the thought, is removed, then the life current will flow. There can be no flowing until you clear up the blockage.

Prophetic Principle #9

Self talk can destroy you.

Saying things to yourself can produce action, positive or negative. Be watchful of your words and thoughts because one day they will break into action. You cannot afford the luxury of a negative thought, or pity party, for these are destructive forces awaiting their moment to unleash their fury in your life.

God lives in a three room house. There is an outer court, an inner court, and a holy of holies. You are the temple of God, and God dwells and walks in you. The only reason you are not seeing the move of God in your life is because of the blockage in your life. God wants to become the Word made flesh in you, to manifest in your flesh.

The spirit of the antichrist will say that Jesus did not come in the flesh. The world is saying, "Show me the supernatural, show me Jesus." They are going to the Ouija boards, soothsayers, and clairvoyants, because they are looking for God. The world is still looking for God because the Church has not shown them God. We have to enter into an identity of knowing Jesus and being joined to Him so that the world can know that when they see us they see the Father.

We must reject the mentality that says, "Woe is me, part of my Christian walk is suffering, so I am continually going through." That is not a representation of God's Kingdom. We have to get to the place where when the world says, "I want to meet God," you should say, "You've just met Him, I am His representative. When you see me, you see the Father, what do you have need of?"

Moses' group couldn't enter in because they looked like grasshoppers in their own sight. How are you seeing yourself? What you perceive yourself to be is

Prophetic Principle #10

You have to change your opinion of your identity.

what you are. You are what you think. When the world says, "Show me, I want to see," you should be able to say, "Just watch me and you will see the image of Christ." Young people don't have to succumb to peer pressure! If they stand, they will discover that their peers will want to become just like them.

Number 3: He spoke to the Israelites to cross. Israel means "to rule as God, or rulership with God." You have to begin to rule with God in order to come into your possession. Joshua 1:2 : *"...unto the land which I do give them, even to the children of Israel."* In the Hebrew it literally says I am giving at this moment as you are preparing to enter. When they prepared to cross the Jordan, the land was already theirs. They hadn't even made it to Jericho.

God is saying that possession is yours the moment you are ready to go down into your death. Just as a seed has to go down into the ground and die before the roots begin to possess that territory, you have to go down to your death before you can possess yours.

God is raising up a generation that is going to have the power over death. You have to go down to your death. The reason many of you are not overcomers,

> **Prophetic Principle #11**
>
> You have to embrace the opportunity to cross your Jordan.

is because you still fear the sting of death.

The generation of overcomers will be those who will willingly go down to death. The people who become successful and achievers are those who just don't worry about what happens. You learn what not to do next time. An unsuccessful attempt is the foundation of the next opportunity. Failure is a mentality. Be a trendsetter. Do something different and stick out. While others are trying to follow paths, you are making new trails. Be a trail blazer---not a path finder!

Joshua 1:3: *"Every place that the sole of your foot shall tread upon, that have I given unto you, as I said unto Moses."*

I believe that this call is still going out because God wants man to have authority over all the earth. The law of dominion is at stake here. He began to tell them what was promised them.

> **Prophetic Principle #12**
>
> The Joshua company will be a people of dominion.

Verse five is a key verse: *"There shall not any man be able to stand before thee all the days of thy life..."*

This actually says "no man" will be able to set himself against you and successfully resist you. Glory! He may set himself against you, but he won't be able to resist you. This is the Joshua company.

Moses and his company are running and fleeing in fear and trepidation. Joshua's company won't have to run. They will stand on God's Word. They will give people the opportunity to test God's servants. No one who has chosen to be God's enemy will be able to set himself against you and win.

Verse 5 continues, *"...as I was with Moses, so I will be with thee: I will not fail thee, nor forsake thee."*

God will not be weak nor relaxed towards you, but rather, He will rule with you. Just as He was strong with Moses, He will be strong with Joshua. He doesn't get old and weak. God doesn't have to retire. God is not way up there, old and ancient, He is as strong as He has ever been. God is saying He will not be weak nor relaxed. The same strength He had with Moses, He will have with Joshua.

So we can face our enemy from a position of strength, knowing that God is commanding Israel-- His people who have rulership with Him. These are the people who are able to perceive and obey His mandate to cross the Jordan and possess the land. When you remove adverse thoughts and the current

Crossing Your Jordan

of the Holy Ghost begins to flow, your perspective of yourself begins to change. You can then cross your Jordan as the present day rulership of God in the earth and occupy your land.

Chapter 3
Possessing The Land

"Be strong and of good courage: for unto this people shalt thou divide for an inheritance the land, which I sware unto their fathers to give them.

Only be thou strong and very courageous, that thou mayest observe to do according to all the law, which Moses my servant commanded thee: turn not from it to the right hand or to the left, that thou mayest prosper whithersoever thou goest.

This book of the law shall not depart out of thy mouth; but thou shalt meditate therein day and night, that thou mayest observe to do according to all that is written therein: for then thou shalt make thy way prosperous, and then thou shalt have good success.

Have not I commanded thee? Be strong and of a good courage; be not afraid, neither be thou dismayed: for the Lord thy God is with thee whithersoever thou goest.

Then Joshua commanded the officers of the people, saying, pass through the host, and command the people, saying, Prepare you victuals; for within three days ye shall pass over this Jordan, to go in to possess the land, which the Lord your God giveth you to possess it."

Joshua 1:6-11

Joshua was ready to act. When God gives you the command, **"Be strong and courageous,"** don't sit there and procrastinate! That is fear! You have to go back down into your Jordan and deal with the fear. Regardless of what others say or think, or even if you don't have the money, be ready to act.

Prophetic Principle #13
Be ready to act when God says "be strong".

If God tells you to start something that has never been tried before, do it. Be in position and start moving. Be ready to act. Moses' company went in and saw that the land was good, but they weren't ready to act.

The Church has merely been looking at the promise of dominion, the land of no more tears, no more crying, no more poverty, and no more sickness as the "Great by and by". I want to tell you something, that land is here! Jesus commanded us to pray," Thy kingdom come, thy will be done on earth as it is in heaven". We're to see to it that His will is done here on earth as it is in heaven through the portion that is allotted into our hands. Stop looking over the promised land as a future possibility and be willing to act today! It's your time!

It's time to get up and move forward! Joshua is beginning to come forth as a new order. It is time to let go of the old ways and cleave to the new ways.

Prophetic Principle #14
The old ways cannot go into the promised land.

God is raising up a people who will not just sit and say they are waiting for things to take place "one of these days". They are going to arise with the understanding that God has told them to take the land. You can get your "pie in the sky" now!

When most people think of heaven, they think of it as a weekend vacation. You don't have to wait to go away, you can experience your heaven here on earth. Once we begin to operate in the principles of God's Kingdom, we will find that the kingdom should be within. Jesus, when questioned about when the kingdom would come, said that some would say it is over here or over there. He said that it does not come by observation, but it is within you.

God raised up Joshua--a man He could speak to and who could lead the people----to bring them into that which He had ordained for them. Then God began to make promises to them. He told them that every place that the soles of their feet tread upon shall be theirs. He told them that no man would be able to stand against them or successfully resist them.

When we move under the anointing and in the Joshua mind set, as a deliverer, our enemy will not be able to withstand us. There are some situations that look like the determining factor has already manifested, and that defeat is inevitable.

God wants you to tell the enemy, "Come on. You can try it, but you can't win." He wants you to challenge the devil. God wants you to get in the position where the devil is not busy seeing your backside, but you are busy seeing the backside of the enemy.

As a Church, we have been retreating. We have been saying, "Man, the devil has been on my case all week long." You have to be of the mind set that, "If the devil comes, God knows that I can handle him. God will not allow me to be tempted above my ability to bear it."

Joshua Generation

Prophetic Principle #15

Hard problems only come to those who are filled with His wisdom.

There is a song that says "God will not put on you no more than you can bear". If the problem has come your way, God knew that you would have the answer and the solution for it. The difficulty is that you don't usually know that you have the wisdom to handle the problem. The problem is not an end to itself, but you should see it as a beginning.

Most of the time, when faced with a difficult situation, we respond, "Oh, my God!" and seek for an exodus out of the situation. Instead, you need to see it as an opportunity to bring something new out of you. Yes, the problem comes, but you can manifest the solution.

When you were in school and they passed out a test with problems on it, they didn't want you to look at the test and say, "Oh, my God, problems." What did they want you to do with them? Answer them! Solve them! Stop looking grievously at your problems and start solving them!

The Joshua company was a company of problem solvers. The Moses group couldn't get any further than addition, and they couldn't take any subtraction. Yet the Joshua company began to deal with algebra.

Possessing The Land

They progressed to geometry and later started moving into trigonometry. You will graduate when you get beyond division and fractions. (Selah! Pause and think about THAT!!)

Now, we are entering into some areas where we are going to be primarily adding numbers, but it will include solving for the unknown. There are some situations that you will be required to find the sum by disclosing unknown factors through faith and wisdom. Some areas you will just have $A + B = 6$, and you have to solve for A and B. It is not apparent, yet the wisdom of God on the inside of you is ready to solve it.

A story was once told about a math problem that was still on the board after the teacher presented it to the class and told them it was unsolvable. There was one kid who came to the class late and didn't hear the teacher say that the problem could not be solved. It was already a proven fact that there was no answer to the problem. He copied the problem off of the board, took it home and worked on it all weekend thinking it was a homework assignment. He returned Monday with the answer to the problem. He came back with the answer because he was not told that there was no answer to the problem.

There are some things that come your way that don't have an answer because you have been told that they can't be solved. Some things people have said you have to live with, but you don't. There are some people who will say, "You have to accept being poor, it's come down two or three generations, all of your relatives were poor." Some say that this is your lot in life and you have to live with it. I want to tell you that it is not so.

Because that little boy wasn't told that problem couldn't be solved, that it couldn't be done, he did it. It is scientifically proven that the bumblebee's body is too heavy for it to fly, yet the bumblebee flies because no one told the bumblebee he couldn't! Even the bumblebee has more sense and faith than some of you. The reason why some of you are not flying with the eagles is because you have been told that you can't fly.

The Moses company could not handle the unknown or the unfamiliar. Every time they were faced with it, they became totally dysfunctional. God could not manifest Himself to them because one of His characteristics is omnipotent. "Omni" means unlimited and "potent" is the root of the word potential. So, God is full of things that have never been seen before.

> **Prophetic Principle #16**
>
> In every situation, God has the unknown factors hidden in the counsels of His will.

We disrespect God when we enter an unfamiliar situation and become overwhelmed by seemingly unconquerable obstacles. God is saying, "Let Me be God." You just trust Me and watch as I unleash something that has never been seen before. As the Joshua company, we cannot be shaken by the unknown.

God is beginning to infuse His people with the Joshua mentality----the Joshua mind-set. He is beginning to raise up a people who are going to say to the enemy, "Come on, try to stand against me. I just want to give you a little word of warning: You won't be able to successfully resist me." These people who are not sitting idly by saying "I'm just waiting for Jesus to come. I figure I'm going to heaven any day now--if I make it. I don't know if I can, but I'm sure gonna try." They don't dwell upon these negative problems and suggestions, drowning in a pool of failure.

This is the way the Moses company reacts. "There's giants in the land. We be not able. This world is a terrible place to live. Pray for us in these last and evil days."

But the Joshua company says, "Where is the enemy? Where are the giants? Let's go to the walled city." The Joshua company will take a people and say, "You are coming with me, but there is one thing that I am asking of you - that you just shut up. Don't say a word."

The Bible says *"Upon this rock I will build my church, and the gates of hell shall not prevail against it."* Jesus said that upon that rock He will build His Church

Prophetic Principle #17

The gates of hell cannot walk.

and the gates of hell shall not prevail. Notice that the gates do not have hands and feet. Satan's kingdom has no business moving towards us. We are to be moving in his direction. Some of us would really like to say to the enemy, "Listen, as long as you don't bother me, I won't bother you. Let's just peacefully co-exist."

One thing that God wants to do is awake us out of our sleep. The enemy is trying to make a statement. We wrestle not with flesh and blood. Do you know what God is saying? Perhaps it is time to awake and make counter moves. What are you going to do about it? The Moses company just looked at how rough and tough the giants were.

God is bringing forth a Joshua company. I hope you are a part of the Joshua company. Joshua 1:6 *"Be strong and of a good courage: for unto this people shalt thou divide for an inheritance the land..."*

God is beginning to tell us it is time to get up on our feet and to take action. The Bible says "be strong and of good courage", I found out that it is really saying to be strong, vigorous, and ready to act. In other words, it was a call to combat readiness. God has been saying prophetically for the last decade to get in line. God is saying to be strong and vigorous and ready to act.

> *"And they rose early in the morning and went out into the wilderness of Tekoa; and as they went out, Jehoshaphat stood and said, Hear me, O Judah, and you inhabitants of Jerusalem! Believe in the Lord your God, and you will be established; believe and remain steadfast to His prophets, and you shall prosper."*
>
> II Chronicles 20:20 (Amplified):

I asked God what He was saying. He said, "There

> **Prophetic Principle #18**
>
> **There is a reward for those who will remain steadfast to the prophet.**

are some individuals going through a shaking, they are going through strange occurrences." It's becoming difficult to persevere. God started to tell me that this will determine who will prosper and who will not. The word "prosper" means "to leap forward." He said there will be some who will leap forward, but that there would be others who will go backwards. There are others weighing in the balance saying, "Oh God, this is more than I anticipated. I want to live. Lord, I'm going to take it easy." Angels go by them and say, "Well, that's one off the list." They sold their birthright for some rest. Just as Esau sold his for porridge.

God is saying that something is going to happen in 1992. Something is going to happen in the economy, something is going to happen to the money. He told us to get out of debt by the '90s. God is preparing us, the Joshua company, for such a time as this.

Prophetic Principle #19

Some of you are asking for your portion without a battle.

God wanted them to be strong and very courageous, ready to act. He wanted to divide for them an inheritance in the land. He wanted to give them their portion. I don't believe they got their portion until they got on the other side. Some of you want your portion without going through the struggle of possessing it. Some of you think it should just be dropped into your lap because you believe - "Oh, praise God, I knew it was coming. It took You a little while Lord, a day longer than I expected." Let me tell you something, you have to pass through something. Those of you who are in leadership, if you are not ready for opposition, you had better move back. God is taking the Joshua company across the Jordan, into the promised land to divide the inheritance.

Chapter 4
A Call to Action

Moses interceded for the people. However, God made Joshua a different type of man. Whenever there was sin in the camp that had to be removed, Moses begged for mercy on the people, while Joshua was ready to say, "Have Thine own way, Lord, have Thine own way." There is a point where you begin to intercede and to minister to the people, but God is raising up a generation that is saying they will not peacefully coexist with their enemies. I believe we are going to see a more militant generation.

Something interesting happened recently while we were in the mall in Miami, Florida. We had a Nigerian brother accompanying us. Generally, as a people, they are really serious about their Christian-

A Call to Action

ity, and their walk with God. In their land, they have to be serious about it or the Moslems or other kingdoms will take over.

We just happened to be walking in the direction of two guys who started using four letter words. All of a sudden, this Nigerian brother said, "Shut up! How dare you speak that language in my presence!"

They looked at him quizzically, and kept walking---but their foul language ceased. The Holy Spirit convicted me and said, "Bernard, how many things do you tolerate in your presence that should not be taking place?"

It's almost like the frog in a pot of water. If you put the frog in boiling water, he will immediately attempt to jump out. If you put the frog in cold water and slowly heat the water, he will stay in there and adapt to the environment until it kills him.

How many of us are adapting to our environment? I believe the Lord did that to show me that we are coexisting with so much nonsense that we know is contrary to the Kingdom of God.

Prophetic Principle #20
We cannot peacefully coexist with our enemies.

If your enemy wants to remain with you, he must serve the same God you serve, he has to do the same thing you do, he must be your servant. No more peaceful coexistence.

I was in a barber shop recently where I told some of the individuals that their music was improper and offensive. They began to protest my statement, so I asked them to listen to the words. After listening a while, they were unable to detect anything wrong with the message. The songs denigrated their humanity, yet because they've adapted to their environment, they've lost the ability to judge appropriately.

That's the way the world thinks. They will take their obnoxious music and play it overbearingly loud, but you, with your passive mentality, will take your Christian music and turn it up just above a whisper so you don't offend anybody. The world can boldly hang their perverted items up in the workplace and flaunt their godlessness in your face, but we will put our little Christian items in the desk drawer.

> **Prophetic Principle #21**
> It's time for us to lose our sense of shame and boldly proclaim the gospel of Christ!

On the trains, buses, and restaurants, the world flaunts their Wall Street Journal. There is nothing wrong with it, but they will have the New York Times in your face, yet there you sit with your little

A Call to Action

Bible, maybe even just the little gospel of John. Are we ashamed of our identity?

The Moslems can be in the street yelling, "Mohammed, speak! Hey, brother, let me talk to you about Mohammed." You say you don't want to talk about it, so they will start to call you all kinds of names and you will just sit there and take it.

How many of us aggressively speak about Jesus? We can shyly ask if we can talk about Jesus, and if they say no, we say okay. That day is over. We must be like the Apostle Paul when he said, "I am not ashamed of the gospel of Christ, for it is the power of God unto salvation."

Joshua was a man with vision. He was a man that God was dealing with. God told Joshua that he needed to be strong and of good courage. He was saying that Joshua was to be vigorous and ready to act. There was no place for him to be hesitant or timid about the things of God.

We are going to have to get to the place where even our young people are not ashamed of our Lord Jesus Christ we are talking about.

They may say, "Yeah, I love the Lord", but are they able to say it outside the church? That's where the tire meets the road. Are they able to go out there and tell somebody who invites them to a worldly party, "No, but I'd like to invite you to come to church with me."

Joshua Generation

Because of the peer pressure today, you have to know that you know, that you know, that Jesus is the Lord of your life.

I remember when I was going to high school. I had met the Lord when I was 15 years old. There was nothing boring about knowing Jesus. He was the greatest Person I'd ever met! I used to go around the high school with my big Bible. I had my books in my book bag and my Bible out. I was always talking to people about Jesus. Who cares about what they thought? We have to get to the place where it doesn't matter what people think! The only thing that matters is what the Father thinks. I was always ready to defend the gospel!

God told Joshua to be ready to act. In verse 7, it says: *"And be thou strong and very courageous, that thou mayest observe to do..."* In other words, Joshua, I not only want you to be strong, I want you to be ready for action. I want you to be a man of action who is always ready.

Prophetic Principle #22

God wants you to be ready for action.

Everywhere you go you are bringing the action with you. When you come on the scene, the atmosphere changes. When you really think about this gospel

A Call to Action

that Jesus preached, some of us are not really preaching the same gospel. Jesus said that when the kingdom comes, it would put mother against father, sister against brother. When you really get that gospel of Jesus Christ in you, you can't peaceably coexist with the enemy.

God told Joshua in verse 8:

> *"This book of the law shall not depart out of thy mouth; but thou shalt meditate therein day and night, that thou mayest observe to do according to all that is written therein: for then thou shalt make thy way prosperous, and then thou shalt have good success."*

You make your way prosperous and you have good success based upon your ability to meditate on the law of the Lord.

Verse 9: *"Have not I commanded thee? Be strong and of a good courage..."*

Notice this is three times already that God has spoken to Joshua and told him to be strong and of good courage. Do you think God was trying to get a message to him?

Sometimes you wonder why God keeps saying the same thing over and over to you. "Well, that's what the prophet spoke over me last year. I'm ready to hear something different this time, I'm ready to hear something else."

God says, "No, you're not, you haven't done step one yet." Has there been those seasons in your life where there has been nothing said or no new direction? That's because you haven't perfected the old direction.

I believe that this time Joshua was ready to say, "Lord, don't you have another word for me other than be strong and of good courage? That's good poetry, Lord, but you're kind of repeating yourself here." The Bible says, "Let it not be as the Pharisees with vain repetition..."

> **Prophetic Principle #23**
>
> There is nothing wrong with repetition, but there is when it is vain.

There are some things you must repeat until you get a mental grasp of it. Eventually the light comes on. It seems as though the light began to turn on in Joshua as described in Joshua 1:10,11:

> *"Then Joshua commanded the officers of the people, saying, Pass through the host, and command the people, saying, Prepare you victuals..."*

When Joshua heard that command about the third time, he took action.

A Call to Action

God doesn't say something because it sounds good, but for us to respond. Your response of, "Oh yeah, you're about the tenth one who came and told us that one..." is an insult. God is saying, "Thick head, I would like to give you the next command, but evidently you're just sitting in a relaxed position." So, the Holy Spirit keeps echoing the same thing over and over.

God repeats Himself, because we haven't gone through the camp and said, "Listen, get your stuff ready. Get your things together, we're getting out of here. God says to move over to the other side. Get your house in order, we are about to move into the promises of God."

God doesn't say, "Wait until I send it, then do something," but when God speaks, He wants you to take the action. We say, "Lord, You do it, and then we will know it was You."

Prophetic Principle #24
God wants us to move by faith.

If Peter would have put one foot out of the boat to see if the water was solid, he wouldn't have walked on it. He had to get out and walk. You know how God wants us to move? Many of us are waiting for a manifestation to move into the next thing God has called us to do, while God is waiting for us to move into it to give us a manifestation. Unless you move by faith, you will die in the wilderness. Faith without works is dead.

When you get ready to sit in a chair, you do not turn around and say, "I hope it's strong. I am going to check it out and confirm whether or not it is strong enough to hold me." You just sit yourself down without considering that somebody could have pulled the screws out of it, or that it was not glued together properly, or whether or not somebody wanted to just play a joke on you. You just sat there by faith. This is the way God wants us to move.

When God speaks, He wants us to move with confidence (just like we would go to sit in a chair without inspecting it). Our response should not be that of unbelief, "Lord, we are not sure that this is you? Send us another prophet to confirm that this chair is really strong enough to hold me up."

Joshua had to be ready to take action. God is calling us to be ready to take action. I know it's comfortable and very easy to get in a relaxed position, but today God is telling us to get up and to take action.

Prophetic Principle #25

What has God told you to do?

A Call to Action

Some of you are sitting there holding your hands, some of you are pacing the floor, saying, "Well, Lord, what's next?" God has already said, "Be strong and courageous."

Nowhere in Scripture does it say that God told Joshua to tell the people to be prepared. It indicates that Joshua understood that if God says, "Be ready to act, get yourself prepared to go across Jordan in three days," then he had three days to get his act together.

Some of us are still saying, "Lord, give me another word. I know you said I am going into business. Show me what business." Instead, you should start doing whatever business your hands know how to do. If you know how to sew, get on that sewing machine and start doing something for one month. If that doesn't work, sew something else the next month.

You have to get in a ready position. You have to give God something to work with. We want God to speak to us, give us a business, the angels to get on the sewing machines to prepare the garments, hang them up, and then go out and sell them for us. You have to be ready for action!

> *"Pass through the host, and command the people, saying, Prepare you victuals; for within three days ye shall pass over this Jordan, to go in to possess the land, which the Lord your God giveth you to possess it."*
>
> Joshua 1:11

The land was already theirs. God said it was theirs. As this reads, as you are going to cross the Jordan, the land is yours. You don't have it until you start taking some action. You have to mix faith with what God says. Oftentimes, the more it looks like you are losing it, the more you are actually moving towards it.

Prophetic Principle #26
You can't be moved by what you see.

A pastor was sharing with me about a certain pastor he knew who went down to the railroad track everyday at 2:00. His staff did not understand why he went. So, one day they followed him. He went down to the railroad overpass for about 10 minutes, then he turned around and went back. His staff told him that they followed him, but didn't understand why he went down there to the railroad overpass everyday and just stood there. He told them he just had to see something moving that he wasn't pushing.

There are some of you who know if you stop pushing in your family that it won't move. You have to be a people of action. When people see you they should see movement. They should see progression. They should say, "My goodness, I saw you last year, but this year you look like you are doing mighty fine.

A Call to Action

I remember how you were three years ago, but I hardly know you now." Well, tell them that if they don't know you now they won't know you two years from now because you will be totally out of reach. If you hang around folks who aren't going anywhere, you will find you won't go anywhere either!

Chapter 5
Men of Valor

When the Holy Ghost begins to move in a particular way, we might as well get ready. God is doing some unusual things. Many people are not even aware that they are in the midst of a visitation. So often we can be right in the middle of the thing.... so near it...that we don't understand the purpose, destiny, or reason why it has come.

The '90s is not only the last decade of this century, but we are closing out a millennium. The year 2000 will be here before you know it. Ten years is not a long time.

God is raising up a new breed of leadership, a new mentality. He is bringing forth a new people. Traditional churches are struggling, groveling, floundering without direction, and stumbling without fresh insight. Many do not even have a handle on what God is saying. They try to maintain the status quo when God is saying something totally different. They are saying "this is how we did it 40 years ago, we want to do it the same way 40 years from now."

God is raising up a people from within a people, and He is just bringing them forth out of the woodwork. Many of you sit in some churches and say you have never seen a church like it. "What are they doing up there? What is all this prophesying? Can all of this be of God?"

Prophetic Principle #27
When God brings a visitation, it begins in confusion.

It begins in misunderstanding. We do not run a popularity contest, nor do we explain anything to anyone. When a baby is born, you don't explain things to it, because it doesn't understand. You have a tendency to just raise the child.

When God began to work in the creation, we saw that darkness was upon the face of the deep, it was void and without form (confusion). The Spirit of God moved upon the face of the deep.

Prophetic Principle #28

Every move of God brings gross misunderstanding.

On the day of Pentecost when the Holy Ghost fell, there were 120 saints reported drunk. They were misunderstood in the visitation of the Lord.

Just as sure as you begin to identify, label, walk and move, you will be misunderstood. Forget about trying to explain. Except the Holy Spirit reveal it to them, they won't see it anyway.

Jesus walked with the two men on the road to Emmaus and they thought they had heartburn. They did not even realize that they were talking to Jesus.

There are people in church services who will feel goose bumps and don't know what it is. They will go out and say they felt something at the church, and don't know what it was. They'll mistake it for being "just a little chilly". They were in the Presence of Jesus and did not even realize it. They sat there with their eyes wide open, but did not recognize Jesus.

"And to the Reubenites, and to the Gadites, and to half the tribe of Manasseh, spake Joshua, saying,

Remember the word which Moses the servant of the Lord commanded you, saying, The Lord your

> *God hath given you rest, and hath given you this land.*
>
> *Your wives, your little ones, and your cattle, shall remain in the land which Moses gave you on this side Jordan; but ye shall pass before your brethren armed, all the mighty men of valour, and help them:"*
>
> Joshua 1:12-14

There was a certain mentality that God was instilling in this generation that was to possess the land. Notice that He was beginning to talk to the men. I think it is a shame when you have to send women and children out to war. He wanted the men. The job was only for the mighty men, the men of valor.

His call was not to the weak men. They told the little ones to stay home. I don't believe they meant the little ones in stature, but the ones who possessed "little minds". They were calling for the mighty men, the conquerors, those who can make decisions under pressure.......the mighty men of valor.

What we have been doing in the Church is allowing the women and the children to go. We say, "You pray, honey, you'll hear from God. You take care of that."

Church, hear what I am about to say prophetically with spiritual ears. I believe that the worst thing that has happened to the Church is that the men have lost their vision as husbands, managers, and providers of the home and allowed their wives to go into the job market.

The roles are all mixed up in the home. I'm not against strong women. I think it is good. I just think that their men have to be strong, also. When the man becomes strong and you get those two together, you have an unbeatable team.

However, if you allow your wife to give eight hours of her time to another man, and she doesn't even give you eight hours a day, her loyalty will become greater to her employer than to the husband God has joined her to.

Your rationale may be this, "We are doing it to get more money, to get more income," but you don't understand the subtle trap of that. It has twisted our families, our culture, and allowed our women to become domineering in our homes. Men can't even get a handle on their households because the wife retorts and says, "I make just as much as you do. Who are you? This is my money, I bought this."

When a wife is in the job market, it makes the husband lazy. He doesn't produce at his optimum level, he leans on her. He has no backbone because he is busy leaning. He is not in a position where he has to seek God and use his faith to sustain his household. He has his wife as a covering so he can pick up hobbies and waste precious, productive hours.

Men Of Valor

If his back were against the wall, it would exalt his faith to another level. Most men can't even envision themselves as the sole provider of their homes, when that is God's vision for them. I know that is the way the world does it, but we are peculiar. Don't misunderstand me, I'm not saying women shouldn't work. Work in the family enterprise, work around your home, make sure it is out of the family.

I believe that God is going to raise the man to his place. The matriarch arises just because the patriarch hasn't taken his place on the throne. There is a clarion call to wake up!! For it is time for action!

Prophetic Principle #29
God is challenging men.

We have to stop warehousing our children. When you are out of the home, somebody else has eight hours with your children. They are spending more hours with your children than you are.

When you come home, you tell them to eat their supper and then get ready for bed. Then, the next thing they hear is to get up and get dressed because it is time to go. The only commandments your children hear from your mouth is eat, go to bed, wake up, and eat your breakfast. Someone else is shaping their personality, someone else is pouring their lives into them. We have to get back to some traditional values! We have to understand we've been lured into a trap.

Single parents are a witness against the double income family. If they are making it with one income and raising children, why do you need two incomes? Now, we are not saying that you should sit around home and twiddle your thumbs when your children are in school. You should be busy doing something. Just make sure that something is not consuming your soul until you are not able to pour into the life of that seed.

We see that these individuals had to pass by. The Bible says that they should pass before them harnessed. When God began to speak to me about the men, I asked what He was saying to my local church. He said, "The problem with the men is that they have not been under My influence." Placing your neck in the harness of the Lord will make you a mighty man.

When God led Israel out of Egypt, the Bible says that they went out harnessed. They went out in ranks, they went out under control. They understood government.

Prophetic Principle #30

It isn't until you are under authority that you can be in authority.

Men Of Valor

"Why does God have me serving under him? I should be the leader of this thing. I don't know why I am here." You don't even have a clue, you can't see, you are blind. The reason God appointed you to serve under authority is, He is trying to harness you for leadership so that you can operate in true authority.

When they left out of Egypt, they were harnessed. They moved in rank and they understood military order. God is saying, "Yes, you have been a part of the Body of Christ, you have been a joy, I understand that, but now I want to speak to you concerning My army. If you are going to do this, you need to move into the army of the Lord. There must be some harnessing."

In the whole episode with Jezebel, the problem was not with Jezebel, the problem was with Ahab. "Jezebel" simply signifies "to be out of control." Ahab should have gotten her under control and harnessed her.

Some domineering women need a good man to come into their lives, harness them and bring some governmental order into their lives. Those who are not harnessed at home come into the church unharnessed. They come with their own problems, an independent spirit, and want to do their own thing. It's not a demon working in them--they just need a man to stand up and harness them. They are out of control.

Joshua Generation

This is why a man has to be able to rule his own house and have his children under subjection. Children have to be harnessed. My daughters try me. I command, "go to bed." They reply, " Okay." Lights flick on and off. They are trying me. It's the same way in the House of the Lord. People come from mixed up, confused families. Some of them don't even know what a real man wielding God's authority looks like.

When they see true authority they buck against it, because they don't recognize it as true authority.

Say whatever you want to say about the Moslem community, but if they are faking it they are doing a good job. Those men look harnessed. They don't go around looking for police patrol, they have their own patrol in their communities. Do you think God is speaking to us? The moslems don't have women out patrolling, they have men out watching on every corner.

What God is calling for is the mighty men of valor to be movers and shakers. These men were harnessed, under control, and witty. You never fight side by side with a fearful man because a fearful man will accidently shoot you. That's why Gideon sent home those who were fearful. We have to become harnessed.

When you aren't harnessed you are out of control. That's the spirit of Jezebel. They start taking charge,

Men Of Valor

but they'd better watch out because the harness is coming. Gideon revival is coming. This revival is so good that if folks asked what is going on, we will say, "Oh, we're in revival this month. This is revival month." Who is the speaker? Jesus. What is a Gideon revival? God is just saying, "Send the boys home."

The brethren were to be armed, all the mighty men of valor, and help them.

Verse 15: *"Until the Lord have given your brethren rest, as he hath given you, and they also have possessed the land which the Lord your God giveth them..."*

In other words, you can't rest until your brethren rest. Let me tell you something about rest. Rest is to

---
Prophetic Principle #31

Rest is not the end of work for man.

---

be the beginning, and then work comes out of the rest.

> *"Come unto me, all ye that labour and are heavy laden, and I will give you rest. Take my yoke upon you..."*
>
> Matthew 11:28,29

When there is a call unto rest, rest is the beginning of true labor. When you are called into His rest, He

Joshua Generation

begins to yoke you. When you come unto Jesus, He begins to place the yoke which is around Him around your neck and yoke you to His purpose.

This is when the song "Where he leads me, I will follow" becomes a reality. If you try to go the other way, that yoke will break your neck. The first thing that happened when God created man was that He rested the following day. The first thing man entered into before work, was rest.

One individual might say, "I've been called. The Lord called me." When God calls you, He doesn't send you away. Those people who say they feel the call of the Lord may be busy trying to get away from Him. They feel they are called to preach, so they want to know where they can go to minister. They are going in the wrong direction.

When the Lord calls us unto Himself. He's saying, "Come here." While He is saying, "This way," you are saying "Huh?" Preach that way? No, you must mean go ye into all..." You don't want to enter into the rest. You are so busy being consumed with ministering, that you haven't entered into rest. This is why many begin to go out and minister and encounter frustration because there has never been that "rest". You have never come unto Him. You have never been yoked to Him.

He is saying, **"Come, so I can yoke you."** When He yokes you, you won't have to send out resumes. You

Men Of Valor

need to hear this. You won't have to go out there and say, "Listen, you need to have me in your church."

I don't send out resumes saying that I am a prophet, that I prophesy word of knowledge, and word of wisdom. I am booked up for the year and have not sent out one resume. When there is a call of God, He calls you unto Himself. He yokes you, and He will open up the door. You don't even have to knock. As you begin to walk, the Red Seas are commanded to part!

We can't do it the world's way. They are knocking on doors saying, "I'm here, let me in." "Who are you?" "Just let me in, I have ministry for you." No, you just come unto Him and enter into His rest. God is the One who raises up, and He is the One who takes down.

God speaks something into your heart. You need to be like Mary. God allowed Mary to carry the baby Jesus because she was harnessed. She had the harness of the Lord on her.

The wives and children were to be kept at home to keep the home intact. The warriors went before their brethren harnessed, and they went armed. They were there to help them enter into their purpose.

Joshua told the wives and children to stay home, but all the mighty men of valor should pass by armed. These mighty men of valor were coming out of the tribe of the Reubenites. Reuben means "behold

Joshua Generation

the son." Reuben was the firstborn of Leah, a man child. He had already given the firstborn his portion, but he said, "Firstborn, before you enjoy yours, I want you to pass before your brethren to make sure they enter into theirs first."

Joshua instructed the Reubenites that they couldn't enjoy their land yet, they had to make sure that their brethren got theirs. He also spoke to the Gadites, who were born out of Leah's maid. Gad means "a troop cometh."

God is speaking prophetically to this generation, to the crack addicts, to the cocaine users, and to issues. He is saying, you better look out because a troop is coming. There is a people that God is raising up who are saying, "We have gotten our inheritance, but we aren't going to enjoy our prosperity, our healing, or our blessing, until we can go out and set others free." A troop is coming!

It is not enough for us to sit behind four walls and wear gold jewelry. It's not enough to wear nice clothes and to look neat. God is saying we are to take our walls down. Whosoever will, let him come.

I heard on the news recently that a church was debating whether to let AIDS victims in. If Jesus would have turned away those with leprosy, which was very contagious, He would have indicated that leprosy was too great for Him to heal.

We, as a Church, the Body of Christ, have the solu-

Men Of Valor

tion. We can't turn away the problem - homosexuals. We don't hate homosexuals, we hate the sin. We shouldn't turn them away, but bring them in so that the Word can set them free. The truth shall make them free!

Bring in the harlot, the drug addict, the drunkard because they are searching and thirsting for something, and we can't refuse to give them the Jesus they are searching for!

There is a craving inside that they are trying to satisfy, a high that they're striving to find. They don't understand that what they really are looking for is the Holy Ghost.

There are those who spend all day in the malls just spending money, not really understanding that they are going to the wrong place. The unrest is inside of them, and because of that, they are searching for satisfaction in things. We have to tell them to stop looking at things, but to come drink of the waters freely given by Jesus Christ, and they will never thirst again.

He means "my Satisfier". A lot of people know of Him and talk about Him, but don't really know Him.

Prophetic Principle #32
What does Jesus mean to you?

Joshua Generation

Nicodemus knew of Him, but didn't really know Him. He woke Jesus up in the middle of the night. He knew Jesus was a teacher. A lot of people know of Him and the things that He did; His miracles, and His teaching.

It is only when you connect with destiny that you know Jesus. It isn't enough to know a Bible story or to know of His works. You must get to know Him and the fellowship of His suffering and be made conformable unto His death.

The reason many people don't know Him is because they don't want to have fellowship in His suffering. What is it going to cost to follow Him? I've been asked, "Have you ever thought of turning back from following Him?" My response is, "No, it never crosses my mind."

Like the disciples, you can be so consumed with Jesus that when He told them He was leaving, they wanted to know where they would go. I wouldn't know where to go. There is nothing else out there for me. If I left Him now I would have no place to go. He is all that I know. I have learned that He is truth, and what is out there is a lie. No, I have nowhere else to go.

This is why the Bible says when you come to Him, He keeps you. Jesus said that those who are in the Father's hand can't be plucked out. If satan can take you out of the Father's hand, that means that satan is stronger than God.

Men Of Valor

Some were never in His hand. All they had were warm bumps. They felt the quickening; they may have babbled a few words in tongues. They may have come to the altar and said they would like to receive Jesus. But they only knew of Him and never really knew Him. If they were truly in the Father's hand, they could not be plucked out. When you meet Jesus, you will be eternally secure.

When this was happening, it was an election process. He voted you in. You think you voted Him in,

Prophetic Principle #33
You have not chosen Him, but He has chosen you.

but He was the One who opened up your eyes so you could see Him and He drew you unto Himself. I don't think about leaving Jesus. I have nowhere to go. When you truly become a disciple of Jesus, you have nowhere else to go.

Joshua also spoke to half of the tribe of Manasseh in Genesis 41:51:

> "And Joseph called the name of the firstborn Manasseh: For God, said he, hath made me forget all my toil, and all my father's house."

God wants to bring a Manasseh into your life. He

gave Manasseh his portion. Notice that it says "God hath made me." I had nothing to do with it, He made me.

A woman in the throes and agony of labor, will loudly declare that she will never have another child again and nine months later she's with child. While you are in labor and those labor pains are coming, you are saying, "This is it. This is it! When this one comes out, I won't be back..." However, when that baby comes and you gather your precious infant in your arms, the joy and love that you experience has a way of making you forget your toil.

He is going to birth a situation in your life that is going to cause you to forget your toil.

Prophetic Principle #34

God wants to birth a Manasseh in your life.

God has a way of making you forget all your toil and all the promises that have been made to you. He has a way of setting you in a new root system. While you are there looking for your roots, He will begin to reestablish you.

Your roots are in Jesus. He has a way of removing the curse. Joseph's brothers didn't know who he was because God made him forget his toil. His brothers

Men Of Valor

knew they had put him through a rough situation, they stripped him of his coat, and left him naked.

Joseph was a mighty man of valor, born of destiny and called for great purpose in his generation. God is yet calling for the mighty men of valor, those who can suffer persecution and be effective under pressure. He is calling those whom He has called unto Himself and harnessed. He is calling those who will venture beyond the church walls and champion the cause of God in a world full of giant problems and giant issues.

Chapter 6
The Joshua Mentality

Joshua began to tell them to prepare victuals. Joshua 1:12: *"And to the Reubenites, and to the Gadites, and to half the tribe of Manasseh, spake Joshua, saying..."*

Verse 15: *"until the Lord have given your brethren rest, as he hath given you, and they also have possessed the land which the Lord your God giveth them: then ye shall return unto the land of your possession and enjoy it..."*

He told them that they were about to go over Jordan and that they needed to know they were going as one body....no group was exempt. As a matter of fact, those who already had their inheritance, were going to lead the rest of them and show them how to get theirs. He wanted to make sure

The Joshua Mentality

everyone understood that the mission was not complete until everyone was in their rightful place.

I believe God is saying the same thing to the Church today. God wants to realign the home and the Church. So, we need to address some of the disorder and inequities.

We need to expand our vision of prosperity to include the entire body. You shouldn't be able to enjoy what you have until you help others get into their place of rest. I can't even enjoy my manhood until you enter into yours.

> **Prophetic Principle #35**
>
> **My manhood isn't fully developed until it is transferable.**

It's not an honor to say, "Well, I'm the only one to enter into God's blessing." It should grieve you. I can't even enjoy a better thing; I would feel a little guilty sharing what God has been doing for me if it is not manifesting in your life.

If Brother Moore is a carpenter, let me make sure he gets a certain number of contracts. Let me help him up, because as I'm helping him up, he'll probably bring about 10 or 12 others with him. This is how a network is supposed to work!

If another brother has a limousine business, let's try to connect him with a dealership so he can purchase his limousines at near cost. That way he can operate a profitable business because we know that he can hire about 20 drivers. Even if we have to pay a little bit more to patronize him we don't mind it because we know that we are investing so others can come on board.

God was eradicating the crab mentality out of the children of Israel, and He is also rooting it out of the Church. "You are a little too high, let me pull you down so you can be on the same level as I am."

No, no, no, it's supposed to work the other way around. "Let me help pull you up!"

Prophetic Principle #36
It isn't the enemy outside we have to be concerned about, but rather, it's the enemy inside.

Have you ever seen crabs in a big tank? They crawl over each other trying to get up pulling each other down in order to get higher. We must see beyond racial, gender, social and economic barriers. God has to open up our eyes to get us to the point where we say, I can't rest until you enter into yours.

The Joshua mentality is one that says "Even though I have my land, I can't rest until you have yours. God

The Joshua Mentality

is moving me forward, and I can't rest until I see you enter into yours". We must uproot that self-centered spirit which has crept into the Church.

The Jews are a good example in this area. They have a strong network with a lot of inside information. They make sure their rabbi lives well. That might be one of the reasons God takes care of the Jews, because they are busy unlocking dreams for others.

You don't ever hear the Jews complain about their rabbi. However, you hear people say, "the preacher gets all of the money." (Now, I wish that were true). That same spirit, that crab mentality, that mind-set, says "I don't want to help him out because I don't want him to get too big. We have to keep him down here with us. Let him struggle a little bit. That way, he will stay nice and humble before Jesus." We must understand that as the leader emerges, so will the people God has set under him.

God wants to destroy that elitist spirit at the roots because that worldly spirit is in the Church. "Now that I have my education, I need to worship with people who are more educated. I want to get into more of a mainline church. We have Dr. So and So here, and Attorney So and So, and Sister So and So from Such and Such, and Dentist So and So who always sits next to me in service."

The spirit of poverty is not going to be broken over the congregation until the pastor prospers, then as shepherd, under the anointing of God, he will lead his flock into greener pastures.

> ### Prophetic Principle #37
> If God has prospered you it is not for show, but to sow.

We have to get away from that type of mentality, we can't forget the way we were. We have to be able to pull others up with us and increase their vision.

Some of us have the spirit of the cupbearer. He got in Pharaoh's house and forgot all about Joseph. He was just glad to get there. He forgot all about God, Joseph, and the dream he interpreted for him - just flat out forgot about him.

Ministries have grown and seen great wealth. When asked, "How did it happen?" The response is usually, "Well, we just prayed and fasted and the Lord blessed." They forget to mention that there was a prophet that passed through there and really ministered, gave direction, and showed them things supernaturally concerning the ministry. They forget all about that. They think that it is a result of their intercession.

"Well, she was a major support. She helped accomplish some things for the Lord. This one over here

The Joshua Mentality

> ## Prophetic Principle #38
> Understand that when you enter into your inheritance, you need to bring others with you.

helped to get all our music together for the House of the Lord, and this one here helped to get all our writing together. They are the ones who made me look literate." We have to learn how to bring others up.

As Daniel was exalted in the kingdom so was Shadrach, Meshach, and Abendnego. He didn't just sit up there when he got in the kingdom and say, "Yeah, just keep those three boys in the fiery furnace. As long as I'm here by myself, I'm the only one. They love me here." We have to get rid of that bad spirit.

God wants us to get to the point where we say we cannot rest until our brethren have entered into their rest.

Chapter 7
The People's Choice

"Whosoever he be that doth rebel against thy commandment, and will not hearken unto thy words in all that thou commandest him, he shall be put to death: only be strong and of a good courage."

Joshua 1:18

This is the people's choice, their decision. This is a proclamation of the people to meet the challenge facing the congregation. They are taking their destiny into their own hands. This is the body regulating itself.

What are the people saying in the Church of Jesus Christ today? God is listening, and I wonder what

The People's Choice

He is hearing! What are we saying in response to the commandment of Joshua? We're called to hearken, to listen attentively, and embrace the idea of being obedient.

Notice that these people weren't making any exceptions when they said "whosoever." It didn't matter if you were having a bit of financial trouble. These people had gone through 40 years of torment in the wilderness because some folks had messed up.

Ten people affected the destiny of an entire nation by returning with an evil report. The Joshua group said that it would not happen again, for whoever rebels will be done away with.

Joshua didn't even have to deal with it, the people dealt with it because their destiny was tied up in the thing. If a critical spirit should arise, they would be dealt with immediately (the people demanded that it be so).

There are some individuals who have attitude problems. You need to go and tell them they are not really with this program and should move on. Some may not think that is walking in love. You can call it whatever you want. The way some people are acting, love would be a swift kick out of the door before they invoke even more of the wrath and judgement of God. Sounds harsh? Perhaps you believe that we're to move in "love" (sloppy agape), leave them alone, and let them corrupt themselves? Those of the

Joshua Generation

Joshua company will understand that their destiny is tied up in this thing!

The people told Joshua he wouldn't even have to deal with it. "You just tell us what to do, we will do it and will be watching those that don't." The people said they would kill those who rebelled, because they are a cancer and they would keep them from entering into their destiny.

If Moses' group had killed those ten spies, they would have been in the promised land. Sometimes it's better to sacrifice the one for the many. Because of the nature of rebellion, we have to get rid of the one to save the many. It's a disease. You would be quarantined for certain diseases. No one could go in or out. They would search out who you were with and quarantine them also.

The response of the people was not a result of Joshua's encouragement, for the people already had this conviction. While they were hurting in the wilderness, they realized why they were in that position and determined not to let it happen again.

Prophetic Principle #39

They resolved to eliminate the rebellion because it destroys vision.

The People's Choice

They encouraged Joshua to be strong and of good courage, to be ready to act. They said, "We will take care of the rest. You just tell us what to do." There was no question of what to do with an Achan. They didn't even have to pray about it.

If we are going to be progressive as a Church, there are some things that we have to do. If you see people around church with a critical spirit, you need to address it. If you don't take action, that means you are in agreement with it. There are some things we must do.

The people said that whoever didn't hear the commandment, whoever didn't obey, whoever has a problem with this thing, we will eliminate them with their problem.

Prophetic Principle #40
A critical spirit will open you up for demon possession or demon oppression.

If you want the enemy to enter in, all you have to do is have a critical spirit.

Peter, by having a critical spirit concerning the destiny and purpose of Jesus, provoked Jesus' rebuke when He said, "Get thee behind me, Satan."

The devil entered Judas, who had a critical spirit, because he didn't think that Jesus was handling the money properly.

Under Moses' administration, things were handled one way. It was something different when Joshua came along.

We need to understand some things concerning the people's choice. God wants to do something in your life. Some of you have no idea of what He wants to bring you into. God has brought you to where you are now so that He can begin to unfold your potential.

Prophetic Principle #41
Great men are simply little men expanded.

God desires to expand you, and challenge you. Jesus was grieved in the story of the fig tree because when He reached into the fig tree there wasn't any fruit. It is not enough for us to have the title and the look, we must produce.

The Church has been all dressed up with nowhere to go. God has been sovereignly reaching into the Church each week for the produce. He is not finding any fruit. He is saying, "It looks good, (they look like they are saints and full of faith), but as I feel the branches, they are empty. You have the right confessions and know the Scriptures, but when I reach in there, faith accompanied by works is needed. It is not coming to fruition."

The People's Choice

Do you really believe God is God, or are the leaves dressed up on the outside on Sunday mornings? Fig leaves with no fruit.

Jesus is saying He is not concerned with the outside dressing, He is looking on the inside of you for the produce. That's why God only dealt with mighty men in Joshua's generation. The boys were sent home because they did not have the ability of the men. They could not handle the weight of responsibility-- the fruit of life was not there.

Are you all dressed up with no place to go? Looking good with no place to go could be very frustrating. The Church is not to be like a car without any gas in it--all engine and no power. All it can do is stay in one spot.

Some churches are on the right track, but aren't moving. The train is about to come, and you will get run over. Stagnant water stinks. If you are in the same place this year as you were last year, you stink. You are supposed to go from glory to glory.

I've learned that the individuals who God makes the promises to are not the same people He fulfills them through.

Abraham was not the same person as he was when the promise was given. He was Abram when the promise was given, but he was Abraham when the promise was fulfilled. The promise was given to Jacob, but fulfilled in Israel. Something happens

Joshua Generation

between the time the promise is given and the time the promise is fulfilled.

We are only at the place where the promise is given and we have to go through some things to get to the place where we are to be when the promise is fulfilled. I am not sure what it is going to take. I do know that it is going to take the Gideon revival.......there has to be some weeding out. Some folks are just scaffolding, they are not a part of the temple. They are not a stone. They show up every week, are externally obedient to every mandate, but they are just tools to build the house. When the structure is up, the screwdrivers, saws and ladders leave.

There are some things God is saying to us as a people. He desires to bring about a change in us, but we still want to stay right where we are. We are saying, "this is a comfortable seat, and I know I'm on the right track." God wants to move you down the track, but you want to stay there.

God made a promise to Moses that he was to be the deliverer of the children of Israel. When Moses did not make the change, God's hand was in Moses' neck. God can make a prophecy to you, and you will die in the wilderness if you don't walk according to His Word and never see that prophecy fulfilled. You shouldn't go around saying it was a false prophecy. No, the thing that was false was when you failed to fulfill your purpose.

The People's Choice

God will not allow a Moses administration to cause his Word to return unto Him void. He will raise up a Joshua generation to possess the land. There is a new spirit going forth in the earth. God is raising up a people that will fulfill their purpose. They will cross their Jordan and possess the land as one body. Each part will work effectually increasing the entire body to the edifying of itself in love.

VIDEO CASSETTES
BY BISHOP E. BERNARD JORDAN

RACIAL ETHICS OF THE KINGDOM
Confronts the intrinsic racism that has permeated Christian doctrine. A Thorough study of the "traditional" teachings of the Church unveils a deliberate strain of racism that fosters white supremacy and eradicates the image of God within the African-American. It was this same strain of religiosity that soothed the consciousness of many and justified the atrocities of slavery in America. This series delineates the patent effects of such doctrine and restores the dignity of all races under God that were created for His divine purpose. 4-Video series $80

FREEDOM: THE WAY OF LIBERATION
A clarification of God's true definition of freedom and the resulting implications of the facade of liberty that continues to enslave the African-American community. The continuous assault of malevolent imagery that society uses to deliberately cripple the function of an entire race of people and deface their cultural legacy actually recreates Jesus Christ, the anointed Deliver of men, into an effigy that is crucified afresh on a daily basis. True freedom will emerge as the traditions of men are dethroned and replaced by the uncompromising Word of God that will cut every insidious lie asunder. This series will offend many who have been blinded by the hypnotic lies that have lulled their purpose to sleep, and challenge others to look beyond the veil of mediocrity and prejudice and behold the beauty of God's original intention towards men. This four-tape series is an unforgettable encounter with past, present and future as it proclaims the manifest destiny of the African-American and the Kingdom of God. 4-Video series $80

A PASSAGE TO LIBERATION
"A Passage to Liberation" is a thought-provoking edict against the dichotomy of society's offer of "Liberation" towards the African-American, versus their true liberty as ordained by God. The ingrained levels of prejudice that are encountered on a daily basis are indicated through the ethical teachings of the Word of God. Your spirit will be stirred to defy the implied boundaries of racial denigration, and thrust into the zenith of your capabilities through Jesus Christ. 4-Video series $80

PREPARATION FOR LEADERSHIP
A scathing indictment upon the insidious racism that permeates American society. Using Exodus Chapter 2 as his premise, Bishop Jordan delivers a powerful comparison between the pattern of oppressive leadership that requires divine intervention in the affairs of men and culminated in the appointment of Moses as the deliverer of Israel with the oppressive leadership that the African-American encounters within society and within the walls of the Church. Frightening in its accuracy, this teaching, though disturbing to the ear, is truly the Word of the Lord for this hour, for there are serious ramifications that the Church must contend with if she is to bring a solution to the crisis of woe in this nation.
4-Video series $80

THE SPIRIT OF THE OPPRESSOR

This series, The Spirit of the Oppressor, by Bishop E. Bernard Jordan, attacks the very fiber of societal influence that manipulates the gospel to justify racial supremacy. The insidious attitudes that permeate the Church are also addressed, for judgment begins in the House of God. By understanding that the Church is called to be the example for the world to follow, this series is powerful in its ability to expose the evil that lurks in the shadows of the "acceptable norm," and echoes a clarion call for deliverance from the lie that masquerades as the truth. Are you REALLY ready for the Word of the Lord?
4-Video series .... $80 also available as a book.

NO MORE HANDOUTS

In this series, Bishop E. Bernard Jordan addresses an inflammatory issue that has been instilled as a mindset within an entire nation of people. The American society has methodically caused generations of African-Americans to become dependent to a system that keeps them in a cycle of expectation that the government will always be their source of blessing. Bishop Jordan delineates the intention of God to bring prosperity to His people, thus charging them to turn their attention from the governmental system and discover the treasure that God has placed in their hands, for God is to be their source! This series is challenging and will force you to use your God-given abilities to thing creatively and generate wealth. You don't need anyone's permission to increase, for God has already decreed that you would multiply and wax exceedingly mighty!! This radical message is for a radical people!!
4-Video series $80

THE CROSSING

Bishop E. Bernard Jordan delivers a powerful teaching that defines the attitude that one must take as they begin to cross over their Jordan into the promised land. The paradigms of the old must be shattered as the image of change comes into view. One cannot embrace a new day loaded with old apparatus that is inoperative; old concepts that only brought you to a place of desperation and frustration. Rather, one must search the Word of God and renew your mind to Kingdom thinking that will bring elevation into your life. This series will sweep the cobwebs of mediocrity out of your life, and provoke you to a higher plane of right thinking that will thrust you into the path of dreams fulfilled. Straightforward in his approach, Bishop Jordan preaches a message that is inflammatory to the lies that have taken residence in your mind, and instills the purity of truth that is the nature of Almighty God. 4-Video series $80

UNDRESSING THE LIE

In this series, Bishop E. Bernard Jordan addresses a crucial issue in the Body of Christ -- RACISM. This series will captivate those who are true lovers of truth, for Jesus Christ is the Truth, and many have hidden Him and His cultural reality from the eyes of many. By conducting a thorough search of the Scriptures, Bishop Jordan identifies the Bible's description of Jesus that has been marred by the lies of those who wished to destroy an entire nation's concept of themselves, instead rendering theology that warped the image of God and denigrated them by teaching that they were cursed. Questions that have wandering in the minds of many for hundreds of years are answered as Bishop Jordan takes a strong stand to unmask the lies that have been masquerading as Truth. 4-Video series $80

LEGACY
In this series, Bishop E. Bernard Jordan expounds upon the African presence within the Scriptures. Combatting the misnomers that Africans were cursed by God and that they had very little to do with the unfolding of Biblical events, Bishop Jordan smashes the veil of delusion to cause the obvious truth to surface. During this season, God is causing a cultural renaissance to emerge. The oppressor of American society has lulled the minds of most people into a stupor of ignorance leaving them landless, powerless, and, once again, easy to enslave. The historical accounts within the Scriptures have been bequeathed as a legacy from our ancestors to proclaim the Word of the Lord against the sophisticated genocide that is affecting the African-American. A nation that ignores its past is doomed to repeat its failures in the future. Bishop Jordan brings clarity and balance to an inflammatory topic that is frequently misunderstood. 4-Video series $80

ECONOMICS: THE PATH TO EMPOWERMENT
This vital tape series by Bishop E. Bernard Jordan and Prophet Robert Brown deals with God's answers to the financial instability that has crippled the strength of the African-American nation. By defining the true motivation behind the onslaught of racism, Bishop Jordan and Prophet Brown give clear answers to the persistent societal obstacles that prevent most people from obtaining the true manifestation of God's intention for prosperity in their lives. The articulate questions that proceed from the heart of the nation shall be answered through the accumulation of wealth, for money shall answer all things. This teaching will expose the subtle racism that affects your financial future, and will provoke you into a mindset that will see obstacles as opportunities so that the full potential of God within you may express in your success!
2-Video series $40

NO LIBERATION WITHOUT VIOLENCE
This series will cause one to Scripturally discern the validity of the message of liberation that echoed through America during the 60's through Dr. Martin Luther King and Malcolm X. By holding their messages up to the scrutiny of the Word of God, one cannot help but conclude whose message was more palatable to society, versus the message that stood in the integrity of the Scripture. Challenging in its content, this series is designed to attack the shackles of passivity and charge you to recognize the brutal realities of today's society. You are called to understand the true liberty of the gospel that Jesus preached. 4-Video series $80

A NEW GENERATION
Bishop E. Bernard Jordan is at his best in this series which portrays the change in one's attitude that must take place in order to attain your maximum potential in God and proceed to your Canaan Land! Like Joshua, one must be ready to be strong and of a good courage as you confront racism in this day. This is a radical message to eradicate error and bring forth the truth! Cutting in its intensity, this series will show you how the Word of the Lord will render you untouchable when you are aware of your purpose!! Bishop Jordan defines the new breed of people that God is raising up that will know the art of war, understand and love their enemy as they embrace the arms of destiny fulfilled.
4-Video series $80

AUDIO CASSETTE SERIES
BY BISHOP E. BERNARD JORDAN

THE POWER OF INCREASE
This radical tape series by Bishop E. Bernard Jordan clarifies the principles of God that will bring increase into your life. For those who seem that they are in a continual financial rut, this series will place keys of deliverance that will thrust you into true prosperity.
4-Tape audio series $20

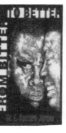

FROM BITTER TO BETTER
Everyone that has ever attained a measure of success has endured the gall of bitterness. There are many individuals whose current situations offend the very essence of their sense of righteousness. Yet God, in His sovereignty, will cause all things to work together for their good, since they are "the called of the Lord." Like Joseph, who endured rejection by his family, slavery, false accusation and imprisonment before he attained His purpose in God, so shall we tread upon the steps of adversity as we climb to the pinnacle of success. This series will thrust you into another dimension in God.
4-Tape audio series $20

KINGDOM FINANCES
How are Christians supposed to prosper as their soul prospers? What is the mindset of success? This series explores the power of money and the responsibility of the Christian to wield his power wisely as an example of good stewardship. These tapes are highly recommended for anyone who has had difficulty maintaining a Godly standard in money management 12-Tape audio series $55

THE FAMILY
The various pressures of corrupt societal influences have challenged the basic structure of the family. Bishop Jordan gives Scriptural premise for the line of authority that should exist in each family, and the development of healthy relationships. An extensive study, this series will revolutionize your home when diligently followed. 4-Tape audio series $20

PRAYER AND FASTING
The significance of prayer and fasting is discussed in this series. The many facets of prayer are discussed, as well as the mechanics of fasting and optimum results, both physically and spiritually. This series is a must for those who wish to develop their spiritual senses to a greater degree.
4-Tape audio series $20
ALSO AVAILABLE IN BOOK

THE HOLY SPIRIT
Is there such a thing as "The Baptism of the Holy Ghost?" "Am I still saved if I don't speak in tongues? What is the purpose of tongues? This series gives a detailed explanation of the identity and purpose of the Holy Spirit in the life of the believer.
2-Tape audio series $10
ALSO AVAILABLE IN BOOK

BOOKS
BY BISHOP E. BERNARD JORDAN

THE MAKING OF THE DREAM
Are you riding the waves to an unknown shore? Is God's will passing you by? Is your God-given vision a dream or a reality? If you aren't sure of your life's destination then you need to hear "The Making of the Dream!" These teachings are remarkable because they will assist you in establishing workable goals in pursuit of success. You God-given dream will no longer be incomprehensible, but it will be touchable, believable and conceivable! $10

THE SCIENCE OF PROPHECY
A clear, concise and detailed exposition on the prophetic ministry and addresses many misnomers and misunderstandings concerning the ministry of the New Testament prophet. If you have any questions concerning prophetic ministry, or would like to receive sound, scriptural teachings on this subject, this book is for you! $10

MENTORING: THE MISSING LINK
Deals with the necessity of proper nurturing in the things of God by divinely appointed and anointed individuals placed in the lives of potential leaders. God's structure of authority and protocol for the purpose of the maturation of effective leadership is thoroughly discussed and explained. This book is highly recommended for anyone who believes that God has called them to any type of ministry in the Body of Christ. $10

MEDITATION: THE KEY TO NEW HORIZONS IN GOD
Designed to help you unlock the inner dimensions of Scripture in your pursuit of the knowledge of God. Long considered exclusively in the domain of New Age and eastern religions, meditation is actually part of the heritage of Christians, and is to be an essential part of every believer's life. We have been given a mandate to meditate upon the Word of God in order to effect prosperity and wholeness in our lives. This book gives some foundational principles to stimulate our transformation into the express image of Jesus Christ. $10

PROPHETIC GENESIS
Explores the realms of the genesis of prophecy...the beginning of God communicating to mankind. The prophetic ministry is examined in a greater depth, and the impact of various areas such as culture and music upon prophecy are taught in-depth. The prophetic ministry must always operate under proper authority, and this factor is also delved into. This book is designed for the mature student who is ready to enter into new dimensions of the prophetic realm. $10

THE JOSHUA GENERATION
A book that rings with the sound of confrontation, as the Body of Christ is urged to awaken from passivity to embrace the responsibility to fulfill the mandate of God in this hour! The Joshua Generation is targeted for those who are ready to look beyond the confines of tradition to tackle the weight of change. Are you a pioneer at heart? Then you are a part of The Joshua Generation!! This book is for you!! $10

SPIRITUAL PROTOCOL
Addresses an excruciating need for order and discipline in the Body of Christ. By aggressively attacking the trend of independence and lawlessness that permeates the Church, the issue of governmental authority and accountability is thoroughly discussed. This manual clearly identifies the delineation of areas and levels of ministry, and brings a fresh understanding of authority and subsequent submission, and their implications for leadership within the House of the Lord. This is a comprehensive study that includes Bishop Jordan's earlier book, Mentoring, and is highly recommended for anyone desiring to understand and align himself with God's order for the New Testament Church. $10

PRAISE AND WORSHIP
An extensive manual designed to give Scriptural foundation to the ministry of the worshipping arts (musical, dramatic, artistic, literary, oratory, meditative and liturgical dance) in the House of the Lord. The arts are the outward mode of expression of an internal relationship with God, and are employed by God as an avenue through which He will speak and display His Word, and by man as a loving response to the touch of God upon his life. This book will compel the reader to deepen his relationship with his Creator, and explore new degrees of intimacy with our Lord and Saviour, Jesus Christ. $20

COMING SOON...
WRITTEN JUDGEMENTS VOLUME III

BREAKING SOUL TIES AND GENERATIONAL CURSES
The sins of the father will often attempt to visit this present generation...however, those who understand their authority in Christ can refuse that visitation!! This series reveals the methods of identifying soul ties and curses that attempt to reduplicate themselves generation after generation. If you can point to a recurrent blight within your family lineage, such as premature death, familial diseases (alcoholism, diabetes, cancer, divorce, etc., then YOU NEED THIS SERIES!!!
Volume I .... 8-tape series.................$40.00
Volume II .... 8-tape series.................$40.00

WRITTEN JUDGMENTS VOLUME I
Chronicles the Word of the Lord concerning the nations of the world and the Body of Christ at large. Many subjects are addressed, such as the U.S. economy, the progress of the Church, the rise and fall of certain nations, and Bishop Jordan prophecies over every state in America with the exception of Ohio. This is not written for sensationalism, but to challenge the Body of Christ to begin to pray concerning the changes that are to come. $10

WRITTEN JUDGMENTS VOLUME II
A continuation of the Word of the Lord expressed towards the Middle East, the Caribbean nations, America, and the Body of Christ at large. Addresses various issues confronting America, such as abortion, racism, economics and homelessness. A powerful reflection of the judgements of God, which come to effect redemption and reconciliation in the lives of mankind. $10

MINI BOOKS

1. The Purpose of Tongues $1.00
2. Above All Things Get Wisdom..................$1.00
3. Calling Forth The Men of Valor....................$1.00

ADDITIONAL VIDEO / AUDIO CASSETTES

This Time Next Year	2 videos - $40.00
Prophetic Connection	4 videos - $80.00
The Power of Money	8 videos - $160.0
Corporate Destiny	4 videos - $80.00
The Anointing	4 videos - $80.00
The Spirit of the Oppressor - expanded	4 videos - $80.00
Boaz & Ruth	4 videos - $80.00
How to Train Up A Child	4 videos - $80.00
The Power of Oneness	4 videos - $80.00
Laws and Principles of the Kingdom	Vol. 1 & 2 - $80.00
Spiritual Protocol (Audio)	4 tapes - $40.00

Order Now by Credit Card and receive 50% off your total order

or

order by Check or Money order and receive 40% off.

ORDER FORM

ZOE MINISTRIES
4702 FARRAGUT ROAD • BROOKLYN, NY 11203 • (718) 282-2014

TITLE	QTY	DONATION	TOTAL

Subtotal	
Shipping	
Donation	
TOTAL	

Guarantee: You may return any defective item within 90 days for replacement. All offers are subject to change without notice. Please allow 4 weeks for delivery. No COD orders accepted. Make checks payable to ZOE MINISTRIES.

Name: _____ Phone _____

Address: _____

_____ Zip _____

Payment by: Check or Money Order (Payable to Zoe Ministries)
Visa • MasterCard • American Express • Discover

Card No.: _____ Exp. Date) _____

Signature (Required) _____